G000068028

LMH Official Dictionary of

Compiled by

L. Mike Henry / K. Sean Harris

LMH PUBLISHING LIMITED

© 2004 LMH Publishing Limited
First Edition
© 2011 LMH Publishing Limited
Second Edition
10 9 8 7 6 5 4 3 2
Reprint 2013
10 9 8 7 6 5 4 3

Compiled by: L. Mike Henry / K. Sean Harris
Cover Design: Susan Lee-Quee
Illustrator: Clovis Brown
Design & Typesetting: Michelle M. Mitchell

Published by: LMH Publishing Limited
Suite 10-11, Sagicor Industrial Park
7 Norman Road,
Kingston C.S.O., Jamaica
Tel: 876-938-0005;
Fax: 876-759-8752
Email: lmhbookpublishing@cwjamaica.com
Website: www.lmhpublishing.com

Printed in China   ISBN: 978-976-8184-63-4

Publisher's Notes

LMH Publishing is pleased to produce a series of books in a series of titles which will treat the Caribbean culture in a serious yet entertaining format.

The first eleven titles in this series are:
- *LMH Official Dictionary of Jamaican Words & Proverbs*
- *LMH Official Dictionary of Popular Jamaican Phrases*
- *LMH Official Dictionary of Jamaican Herbs & Medicinal Plants and their uses*
- *LMH Official Dictionary of Caribbean Herbs & Medicinal Plants and their uses*
- *LMH Official Dictionary of Sex 'Island Style'*
- *LMH Official Dictionary of Sex 'Island Style' Vol. 2*
- *LMH Official Dictionary of Jamaican History*
- *LMH Official Dictionary of Caribbean Exotic Fruits*
- *LMH Official Dictionary of Jamaican Religious Practices & Revival Cults*
- *LMH Official Dictionary of Bahamian Words & Proverbs*
- *LMH Official Dictionary of Popular Bahamian Phrases*

As this series cannot be complete without the response of our readers we implore you, our readers, to voice your opinions, comments and observations which we will take into consideration when publishing new editions.

I hope you enjoy our witty and innovative series. See you next time.

Mike Henry
Publisher

Abbreviations used in the text

adj.	adjective
adv.	adverb
conj.	conjunction
interj.	interjection
n.	noun
v.	verb
phr.	phrase
prep.	preposition
pron.	pronoun
illus.	illustrations

Introduction

Sex. Most people talk about it and everyone at least thinks about it, whether they would like to admit it or not. Sex plays a major role in all Caribbean cultures. It is evident in the skimpy and provocative fashions of the dancehall; and the revealing and colourful costumes used at the various Caribbean carnivals.

Sex rears it's head in Caribbean music, whether its the slow seductive sounds of roots reggae, the pulsating hardcore and often explicit sounds of dancehall; or the sexually liberating and energetic sounds of soca music, that prompts one to gyrate like crazy and lose all inhibitions.

The colourful slang used in the islands of the Caribbean makes talking about sex a very humorous undertaking. The words and phrases we come up with are quite creative; some are derogatory, others hilarious but they all have that distinct island flavour.

This book takes a brief look at the jargon, beliefs and practices related to sex from a Caribbean standpoint. The journey through this book is sometimes risquÈ, sometimes ridiculous (see sexual myths & legends), definitely informative and always entertaining. Enjoy the ride!

A Brief History Of Sex

Any research of the topic sex would show that it has been with us from Adam and Eve's venture into the Garden of Eden. Indeed the Rock Paintings of the Sahara (dating from 4-5000 B.C.) shows several drawings depicting early man cohabitating quite flagrantly.

The early inhabitants of Mesopotamia - the Babylonians, were one of the first to be called immoral, seeing that they produced the earliest recorded forms of erotica; a carved table depicting alternative copulatory poses. The earliest known collection of (porno) hieroglyphics and adult papyruses have been found in the Nile Valley.

Indeed the Egyptian Kings were not unknown to choose as a child bearer, in order of preference, the King's mother, his sister, his daughter.

But the civilization who produced the greatest variety of erotic objects d'art were the Chinese. Their pottery, statuettes, jewellery and coins show men and women fornicating in every conceivable position; with each other, with beasts in the field and with themselves. In fact the Taoists claimed that immortality could be achieved by one's prowess between the sheets.

The Greeks on the other hand felt that sexuality was a gift from the Gods and should be indulged in freely.

History records brothels in the eastern Mediterranean 2000 BC, but it was the Athenians who first brought it under state control and made it subject to a purchase tax. The Greeks also bought homosexuality out of the closet.

The Roman Empire in its heyday sought to make sex a more civilized activity but its decline led to quite weird and extreme actions, including the decree which allowed executioners to rape victims prior to killing them.

The early Christians sought to bring a modicum of control and so urged monogamy and fidelity as expressed by the religions of today; but this did not prevent the participation of some Popes from some sexual recreation one such was John XII and Leo VIII.

The Medicis and the Borgias invited in the return of incest and youth perversion, and the Louis Dynasty took sex to its heights, culminating in Louis XVI's piece de Resistance the Palace of Versailles, where dozens of young girls were retained for his delight at a cost to the French taxpayer.

In Britain, the Normans allowed the deflowering of spinsters in the eve of their marriage by the Lord of the Manor and landlords could claim payments in the form of sexual favours. In fact James 1 was a known bi-sexual that carried on a quite open affair with George Vilbers.

The Victorians ushered in the new era of sexual hang-ups, making sex a duty not a pleasure so that sex was now merely for populating; and masturbation would lead to blindness and fornicators would go to hell.

Despite this, the era led to sado-masochism and pedophilia, and the 1800s saw an explosion of brothels specializing in children, and a surge of flagellation and bondage, and so to today's world and the morals of island sex.

Today we have now seen the churches beginning to accept same sex marriages and gay bishops. The surge of dancehall and hip hop music, which in most of its forms, both glorifies and condemns different forms of sex; and the use of the internet has expanded the global reach of pleasurable pastime, perhaps making Freud's analysis statement a Truism.

Anaconda, *n.* For those men who are well endowed you possess an 'anaconda'. Such men have no problems with the ladies. *(illus.)*

Aids, *n.* The only answer to which is self protection – Use a condom.

"Anaconda."

B

Backshot, *v*. This is when the man penetrates the woman from behind. Some women fear this position as they find it to be painful. Needless to say most men love it.

Back yuh fist, *v*. phr. To 'back yuh fist' is to masturbate. They say it's the best form of birth control and disease prevention, however it's usually men who cannot for whatever reason get a woman, who resorts to 'backing his fist'.

Baggie, *n*. Panties.

Batty, *n*. Ass, bum or backside. Big 'batty' women are a much loved Jamaican commodity.

Batty man, *n*. phr. A homosexual.

Batty ridah, *n*. Those very short shorts worn by females who love to show off their rear end. *(illus.)*

Bedroom bully, *n*. phr. A man who knows how to handle his business in the bedroom.

Big ole gal, *n*. phr. An extremely derogatory term used in reference to a woman whose vagina is loose. To be fair to the ladies however, there are some men who after an embarrassing sexual episode resort to calling the woman a 'big ole gal' in order to make himself feel better.

Big up, *n. (Bahamian)* To get pregnant.

Bingo baggie, *adj. phr.* Refers to those huge panties worn by most fat women.

Boonggy, *n. (Bahamian)* God bless the woman with a big 'boonggy' as that means she has a large rear end.

"Batty ridah"

Boots, *n*. Condom; Rubber. A necessity in these serious times of sexually transmitted diseases. "Mi nuh lef my boots!" I always carry condoms.

Bow, *v*. To perform oral sex.

Bow cat, *n. phr*. One who performs oral sex. Term was made popular by a local hit song.

Bruk out, *n. phr*. A female who used to be quiet and innocent and starts to become loose and promiscuous has 'bruk out'.

Bubby, *n. (Bahamian)* Ladies, if a man tells you that you have nice, firm 'bubbies', he is complimenting you on your breasts.

Buddy, *n*. No this does not mean friend. This is the penis.

C

Cabin stabbin', *v*. phr. To have sex. The term was made popular by an old local hit song.

Chi chi man, *n. phr*. A homosexual.

Chiney brush, *n*. Liquid which is brushed onto the penis to increase staying power.

Chups, *v*. Kiss. *(illus)*

"Chups"

Cock it up, *v. phr.* When a woman 'cock it up' and give you, you're about to have sensational sex with her in a seemingly impossible position.

Cocky, *n.* Another term for penis.

Coochie, *n.* The vagina.

Coochie daddy, *n.* A man who has a reputation of being able to sexually satisfy the ladies.

Crabbie, *n. (Bahamian)* Also known as the vagina.

Dash way belly, *v. phr.* To have an abortion. Rape aside, women who 'dash way belly' are generally looked down upon.

Dicky, *n.* Yet another term for penis.

Doggie, *n. (Bahamian)* Opposite of 'crabbie'. Yes, this is the penis.

Dugu dugu, *v. phr.* To have sex. Usually used only by people from the deep rural areas.

Dutty gal, *n. phr.* A woman who sleeps around.

Eat unda sheet, *v. phr.* To perform oral sex. Men who 'eat unda sheet' are often ridiculed by their peers.

Elty baddy, *adj. phr.* Healthy body. A woman with an 'elty baddy' is one who is very voluptuous. *(illus)*

Empress, *n.* A Rastafarian woman or any woman who conducts herself in a virtuous manner.

"Elty baddy"

F

Fambly ram, *n. phr.* A male who commits incest. These men, when exposed are usually beaten and exiled from their communities, especially in the rural areas.

Fat till it buff, *adj. phr.* Used to describe those vaginas that are extremely plump. *(illus.)*

Feature yuh ends, *v. phr.* Ladies, when a man tells you he wants to 'feature yuh ends' he wants to have sex with you.

Foot pon shoulder, *v. phr.* This is when the woman is positioned so her feet are on the man's shoulders during sex.

Force ripe gal, *n. phr.* Refers to a young female who acts like she is a grown woman. Such females are usually the ones whose bodies develop at a very young age.

Full a mout', *adj. phr.* If you're trying to tell a woman what you will do to her sexually and she tells you that 'yuh full a mout', you are all talk and no action.

"Fat till it buff"

G

Gallis, *n.* A male with many girlfriends and many sexual conquests under his belt.

Gi mi piece, *v. phr.* When a man tells a woman to 'gi mi piece', he's asking for sex.

Gi yuh bun, *v. phr.* To cheat. The man who doesn't have a clue that his girl is giving him 'bun' when it is obvious to everyone else, is quite the laughing stock of his community.

Glamity, *adj.* Vagina that has the 'glamity' is considered good. 'She ave de glamity!' Sex is great with her.

Go go wine, *v. phr.* To move the waistline in a sensuous and sexual manner. The kind of movements men go to strip clubs to watch. Happy the woman who can do this in bed as her man will undoubtedly be home more often than not.

Grine, *v.* Telling a female that you would like to 'grine' her, means that you would like to have sex with her.

Ground shovel, *v. phr.* This is a sexual move, whereby the man penetrates the woman in a movement similar to that of scooping up something with a shovel.

Gun inna baggie, *n. phr.* A woman who has 'gun inna baggie' is infected with gonorrhea. The term was made popular by a local hit song.

Good 'ole a dweet, *adj. phr.* When a woman declares that is 'good 'ole a dweet' she is stating (in a very vulgar fashion) that she can keep any man because her vagina is 'good'.

H

Haas tonic, *n*. Horse tonic. A drink that is believed to increase virility in men. *(illus.)*

Hackle mi baddy, *v. phr*. When a woman tells you that she wants you to come 'hackle mi baddy', gear up because she wants you to have sex with her.

Hile a ride mi, *adj. phr*. To be horny.

"Haas tonic"

Idiat bwoy, *n. phr.* For a woman to refer to a young man as an 'idiat bwoy' means that she considers him to be a total klutz in the bedroom and it can also mean that she considers him beneath her standards.

If yuh coop did clean, de cock would not stray, *phr.* If the sex was good, the man would not cheat.

Joe grine, *n*. This is the name given to the unknown man who your girlfriend or wife is cheating on you with. *(illus.)*

Jook, *v*. To stick. Also used to refer to sexual penetration. 'Mi jook har long time man!' One might be heard bragging to a friend.

"Joe grine"

K

Kill mi wid it, *v. phr.* When a woman tells a man to come 'kill mi wid it' she wants him to have sex with her until she can't take it anymore.

Knock up, *adj.* She 'knock up' means that she is pregnant. 'Mi hear seh yuh knock up Lisa.' I heard that you got Lisa pregnant. *(illus.)*

"Knock up"

L

Length an' strength, *v. phr*. To give a woman the 'length an' strength' is to have sex with her long and hard.

Lizard lap, *v. phr*. Have you ever seen lizards mating? Well Jamaicans have utilized that position in the bedroom, hence the term 'lizard lap'.

Long an' tall, *n. phr*. See 'Anaconda'.

Love punani bad! *v. phr*. A declaration of the adoration most men have in their hearts (and loins) for the female anatomy. It's also the chorus for a local hit song.

M

Mampi, *n.* An extremely fat woman.

Mi nature rise, *adj. phr.* To have an erection. 'Mi nature rise when she come inna de room.' I had an erection as soon as she came inside the room. *(illus)*

Miss kill an' bury, *n. phr.* This is the term given to women who pride themselves on their sexual prowess. They are confident that they can have sex in any position and can accommodate any penis, regardless of size.

Mo gal, *n. phr.* More girls. An expression used by young men who think it's cool to have lots of women.

"*Mi nature rise*"

Neegle yeye pum-pum, *adj. phr.* Used to describe vagina that is tight. Hence the anology needle eye.

Nice fi jook, *adj. phr.* A woman that is 'nice fi jook' is good in bed.

Ole fyah stick easy fi ketch, *v. phr.* When old lovers meet, sparks might fly.

Ova de dicky... *n. phr.* When two women are seen fighting, it is usually assumed that they are fighting over a man. So an observer might comment, 'Ova de dicky de girls a gwaan bad!' Popularized by a local hit song.

Play numba two, *v. phr*. To have anal sex.

Pum-pum, *n*. The vagina.

Pum-pum bush, *n. phr*. Pubic hair (women).

Punani, *n*. Yeah you guessed it, another term for vagina.

Punani tegareg, *n. phr*. See 'bedroom bully'.

Punni printa, *n. phr*. This is the name of those sexy, skimpy shorts that some women wear to show of their asset.

Quarm, *n. (Bahamian)* To walk and swing one's hips seductively. Men seen 'quarming' had better be fast runners as they could very well be chased and given a sound beating.

Renkin' meat, *n.* An unflattering term for vagina.

Rent-a-dread, *n. phr.* These are the Rastafarians that can be seen profiling with female tourists (usually white) at most tourist destinations in Jamaica. *(illus.)*

Roun' like English poun', *adj. phr.* To tell a young lady that she is 'roun like English poun' is to compliment her on her physique. Meaning she has a nice shape.

Rubbas, *n.* Condoms. See 'boots'.

Ruff ridah, *n.* Rough rider condoms. Brand of choice for many Jamaican men.

Run de coochie red, *v. phr.* To 'run de coochie red' is when a man has fully satisfied his partner sexually.

"Rent-a-dread"

S

Shuga cane, *n*. Sugar cane. Men who have the 'shuga cane' know how to please the ladies.

Shrivel up wood, *n. phr*. 'Mi nuh want nuh shrivel up wood man ahoa!' A young woman might proclaim to an old man who is checking her out, much to his embarrassment. *(illus.)*

Siddung pon it, *v. phr*. When the woman is on top during sex.

Skin out an' wine, *v. phr*. When a woman 'skin out an' wine', she is putting on the moves in the bedroom.

Spanish fly, *n*. Liquid which is said to be an aphrodisiac. Some men resort to using this as a means of getting sex from women. They pour the liquid into the unsuspecting female's drink, which then gets her in an extremely aroused state, at which point the man then takes full advantage. Men, this is rape, so don't think about it.

Stab up de meat, *v. phr*. When a man is having sex with a woman he is 'stabbing up de meat'.

"Shrivel up wood"

Stamina daddy, *n.* A man who has a lot of sexual staying power. The kind of man most women require.

Stone, *n.* A hard object (resembles a stone) which is rubbed onto the penis to increase staying power.

Suck wood, *v. phr.* To perform fellatio.

T

Tan pon eh long, *adj. phr.* Used to describe a man who has tremendous staying power during sex.

Tear dung her wall, *v. phr.* A man who is overheard bragging that he has 'tear dung her wall', has just had sex with a female and is quite pleased with his performance.

Tick nuh rass, *adj. phr.* A woman who is 'tick nuh rass' is well endowed in the thighs and buttocks. As you can imagine, these women have no shortage of admirers. *(illus.)*

Tight undaneet, *adj. phr.* Tight underneath. See 'neegle eye pum-pum'.

"Tick nuh rass"

UV

Unda mi high grade, *adj. phr.* To be under the influence of very potent marijuana (Hence the term high grade). Some men, particularly those from inner city communities, love to smoke marijuana before sex. *(illus.)*

Unda mi watas, *adj. phr.* For some Jamaican men it is a rule to have a few drinks before having sex. Guiness Stout being the popular beverage of choice as they think it increases stamina.

"Unda mi high grade"

Wata yuh garden, *v. phr.* Ladies, when a man indicates that he wants to 'wata yuh garden', he wants to have sex with you.

Wheel barrow, *v. phr.* A sexual position where the man penetrates the woman from behind while holding onto her thighs. She balances on her hands while they move in a fashion similar to that of pushing a wheel barrow.

White liva gal, *adj. phr.* Used to describe females who are sexually insatiable. Caribbean women who are of Indian descent are believed to have 'white liva'.

Wickedest slam, *adj. phr.* Girls that have the 'wickedest slam' are great in bed. Girls from the ghetto are rumored to have the 'wickedest slam'.

Wood, *n.* You can't use this 'wood' to make furniture but you can use it to make babies. Yep, this is the penis.

Wuka man, *n. or adj.* Any man who has no problem satisfying the ladies in bed is a 'wuka man'.

Wutliss bwoy, *n. or adj.* This is the opposite of 'wuka man'. A 'wutliss bwoy' is one who cannot hold his own in the bedroom. He either ejaculates too quickly or is just generally clumsy in bed.

Yuh dun know, *n. phr.* You understand. (A statement).
'Yuh dun know seh mi love yuh baby!' You know that I
love you baby!

Sexual
Myths & Legends

COW COD SOUP
This soup is made with the genitals of the male cow and is widely believed to enhance a man's sexual performance.

LEAF OF LIFE
Legend has it that the leaves of this herb placed over the door of your loved one, will tell you if your lover has been faithful. If a new plant grows from each notch, your lover has been loyal. The amount of notches that do not produce a new plant indicates the number of times your loved one has been unfaithful.

MANNISH WATER
This is a soup made with a goat's head and it is reputed to increase a man's virility.

MONOGAMY
It is said that if a man has only one sexual partner for a long period of time, it will cause him to lose his nature.

NYMHOMANIACS

It is said that people of Indian descent are sexually insatiable (see white liva). Most Indian women are offended by this notion and stoutly disagree.

PAPAYA TREE

It is believed that if a young boy beats his penis on the trunk of a Papaya tree, it will cause his penis to grow to a huge size when he gets older.

SOURSOP JUICE

It is believed that if a man regularly drinks Soursop juice, it will cause his sperm to be thick and also increase his sperm count.

Sexual
Aphrodisiacs & Enhancers

CHINEY BRUSH
This liquid, when brushed onto the penis is said to increase staying power.

CONCH
Conch is believed to be a potent aphrodisiac and is also quite delicious. It can be eaten raw in 'conch salad', deep fried in a batter, or used to make 'conch soup'. However, conch is said to be most potent when eaten raw.

GUINESS STOUT
This drink is a favorite of most Jamaican men as it is reputed that drinking a couple bottles of Guiness before having sex will increase their sexual stamina.

JACK HAMMER
This 'roots juice' which is found in Jamaica, allegedly increases the supply of blood to the penis and allows one an hour and a half before ejaculation occurs. It is made of Irish moss, linseed and peanut.

MARIJUANA

Some Jamaican men, particularly those from inner city areas will not even attempt to have sex before smoking a 'spliff' as they are firm believers that marijuana enhances sexual performance.

OKRA PUNCH

This is a drink made of okra, peanut, oats and suppligen all blended together. Some people add other ingredients as well. Okra punch when consumed is reputed to induce sexual desire.

STEAM FISH & OKRA

This is a well loved dish in Jamaica and it is believed that a meal of steam fish and okra is good for the back (men) and will enhance sexual performance.

STONE

This hard object, which resembles a small stone, is rubbed onto the penis to sustain an erection for long periods. It is quite popular with most men.

VIAGRA

These pills aid men who have trouble getting or maintaining an erection. Viagra has given millions of men (both young and old) a new lease on life. However, a word of advice to any young man who is considering using viagra - do so discreetly as you will most certainly become the butt of many a joke.

Sexual
Oddities & Notables

ANCIENT

King David and King Solomon
David had 8 wives and 20 concubines. Solomon had 700 wives and 300 concubines.

Chou H'sin and Yang Ti
Chou H'sin was said to frequently entertain 10 women in one session and invented his own position (sex standing up). Yang Ti was emperor of the Sui Dynasty had one queen, 2 deputies, 6 consorts, 72 royal occasionals, 3000 handmaidens; all to respond to his sexual needs.

Messalina
The wife of Emperor Claudius serviced 50 partners in one session and led to nymphomania being referred to as "Messalina Complex".

Cleopatra
She improved on Messalina's number by using her mouth and performing fellatio on 100 Roman soldiers in one session.

Cassanova
Expelled from a seminary, he proceeded to copulate with hundreds of women of all size, shape and form which he recalled in great detail.

Catherine the Great
Married at the age of 16, she used her status to demand the favours of any man she desired and to make them perform sex at her command.

Feador Vassilet
She gave birth to 16 pairs of twins, 7 sets of triplets, 4 sets of quadruplets - 69 children in all.

MODERN

Marilyn Chambers
She starred in the landmark porno film, 'Deep Throat' which was the watershed for films in the adult genre.

Henry Miller
He is one of the most celebrated erotic writers, known for works such as 'Nexus' and 'Sexus'.

Jonah Falcon
He is alleged to have the world's largest penis (documented). His penis is 9.5 inches when flaccid and 13.5 inches when fully erect.

Playboy Magazine
Founded by Hugh Hefner, Playboy magazine was the first adult magazine to be accepted in the mainstream.

Sex Funnies

BAJAN HANDJOB

A Bajan couple was at the movies. Said the girl to her boyfriend, "The man next to me is pulling his penis." The boyfriend replied, "Take no notice. Just ignore him." She then said, "How can I? He's using my hand!"

MARRIAGE NIGHT SEX

Two proud Trinidadian parents looked on as their three daughters all got married on the same day. That night, their parents listened at their bedroom doors and heard the first daughter laughing, the second crying and the third silent.

In the morning, the mother took them aside one by one and asked them to explain.

"Well," said the first, "You always told me to laugh if something tickled me."

"Well," said the second, "You always said there was no shame in crying if something hurt me."

"Well," said the third, "You always said it was rude to talk with my mouth full."

HI-TECH ANTIGUAN

Three businessmen, a Japanese, an American and an Antiguan were sitting naked in a sauna. Suddenly there was a beeping sound. The American pressed his forearm and the beeping stopped. The others looked at him questioningly. "That was my pager," he said. "I have a microchip under the skin of my arm."

A few minutes later a phone rang. The Japanese fellow lifted his palm to his ear. When he finished, he explained, "That was my mobile phone. I have a microchip in my hand."

The Antiguan felt decidedly low tech, but not wanting to be outdone, he decided he had to do something just as impressive. He stepped out of the sauna and went to the toilet. He returned with a piece of toilet paper hanging from his ass. The others raised their eyebrows and stared at him. The Antiguan finally said, "Well, will you look at that, I'm getting a fax!"

RARE CONDITION

A Jamaican man was sitting next to a woman on a plane. The woman sneezed and then used a piece of tissue to gently wipe between her legs. The Jamaican, not believing what he just saw, said to himself he must be hallucinating. The woman sneezed again and proceeded to wipe between her legs. The Jamaican was getting turned on by the woman's actions and could not take it anymore.

He turned to the woman and said, "Ooman, yuh a try fi drive mi crazy?" (Woman, are you trying to drive me crazy) She replied, "Oh, I'm sorry to make you uncomfortable but I have been diagnosed with a rare condition. Everytime I sneeze, I have an orgasm." The Jamaican, now feeling sorry, asked the lady, "So what yuh tekking for it?" (So what are you taking for it) The woman replied, "Black pepper."

THE RASTAFARIAN

A Rastafarian was being interviewed by a Canadian reporter. She said to him, "Hey, I've heard that 95% of all Jamaican men eat pussy, is that true?" The Rastafarian replied, "I and I don't do them things dere, I and I respect I Queen." The reporter then said, " Hey, I've also heard that the other 5% of Jamaican men are homosexuals." The Rastafarian scratched his beard and said, "Yuh haffi go squeeze I and I back inna de 95% den!"

Animal Facts

HYENAS
Hyenas are the hermaphrodites of the animal kingdom. Some female hyenas have a psuedo-penis.

IGUANAS, KOALAS AND KOMODO DRAGONS
They all have two penises. (Lucky bastards)

OCTOPUS
An octopus has three hearts. Guess they're pretty romantic huh?

PIGS
A pig's orgasm lasts up to 30 minutes.

SWAN
Swans are the only birds with penises.

WHALE

A blue whale's penis measures up to 6 meters. A nursing mother produces over 50 gallons of milk.

Helpful Herbs

CHAMOMILE – This is a good tonic for all the female organs. It regulates and brings on menstrual flow and relieves uterine cramps.

CHANEY ROOT – This herb is used in the treatment of syphilis.

COCOA – The cocoa oil, known as cocoa butter can be used on sore breasts and genitals, as well as in the vagina and rectum to relieve irritations.

COCONUT – A tea made of the roots will stop menstrual hemorrhaging and help treat venereal disease. Eating the inside bark behind the jelly is said to strengthen the back and the sperm.

MAN PIABA BUSH – A tea made of the can be used to strengthen the male reproductive organs.

MOTHERWORT – Improves blood flow to the female organs.

NETTLE – Nettle tea or the fresh juice will promote the flow of breast milk and will also increase menstrual flow.

OBEAH BUSH – This herb relieves indigestion in pregnant women.

PARSLEY – Fresh sprigs of parsley eaten after a meal will sweeten the breath.

PRICKLY PEAR – A tea made of the root is used in treating gonorrhea.

TRUMPET TREE – The tea can be used to expel the placenta after childbirth.